JOHN MARTIN
COLLECTED POEMS
VOLUME 2: GIN-SHOP MUTTON

Published by Bysshe-Mendel Verlag

bysshemendelverlag@gmail.com

Copyright © John Martin 2014

John Martin asserts his moral right to be identified as the author of this work

ISBN 978-0-9930889-1-9

Printed and bound by Short Run Press Limited, Exeter

All rights reserved. No part of this publication may be reproduced, stored in a retrieval system, or transmitted, in any form or by any means, electronic, mechanical, photocopying, recording or otherwise, without the prior permission of the publishers.

GIN-SHOP MUTTON

John Martin

Bysshe-Mendel Verlag

αἰσχύνομαι μέν, ὦ γυναῖκες, εἰ δοκῶ
πολλοῖσι θρήνοις δυσφορεῖν ὑμῖν ἄγαν.
ἀλλ᾽ ἡ βία γὰρ ταῦτ᾽ ἀναγκάζει με δρᾶν,
σύγγνωτε

Sophocles

SUCCES D'ESTIME

Amongst the romantic bric-a-brac,
seaside souvenirs of a reality never believed in,
masking springs of love and levitation
between the stopped clock and the draped mirrors,
hydraulic device, presupposition of the well,
despairing swindler humps his bag of tricks,
sets out his vulgar lies for the slumming certain,
with pristine display of emotion's stock-in-trade
faking responses to their fantasies:
batters the drunken moth against the flame
and the worm starts its cyclic spinning.
These were passwords to the shattered mirror
and the world behind it, where consequence
comes first without connections, as in dreams –
conceptual revenants endued with consummation.

Dissembling like mad, identity skulks about
waiting for cues to reveal itself
out of a secret trapdoor no-one suspected;
hamming it up and histrionic to the last,
thick with greasepaint and grief,
desire stalks the wings on the rampage,
ranting of passion, script in pocket –
who understudies love, senescent heart-throb,
last of the heavies, not to be confused
with appetite, whose monosyllabic butler sleeps it off
between entrances; upstaging them all,
by listening with exaggerated eagerness,
vanity conspicuously underplays,

with studied timing; a listless ceremony
of habitual terror and routine indifference.

They were keys we kept locked up against he come,
as come he would, rising like the astral body
out of the rock's fossil heart,
soaring above the trapeze wire,
scorning the customary exposition.
Solo on the revolving hurricane
before revulsion sets us down to earth,
the fairground mercenaries send us
whirling, whirling through the inescapable
reiterations of our first love.
Many a latter-day face recalls that melting,
but there is no way to grasp the flesh –
the circuits of your recumbent pleasure
light up like a disdainful constellation,
convulsive efflorescence of genetic coral,
generative spasm of spreadeagled frog,
the senses sparkling like a cartridge quickly spent
in the afterglow of extinct embers.

For the most part it's an idle rehearsal,
half the actors late and nobody word-perfect,
least of all me, drying continuously,
making it up as we go along, costumes and
soliloquies mislaid, appearing naked on stage
as in the nightmare, exposed to mockery and shame.
Can this affected coarseness really convince?
I rake my halo like a gangster's trilby,
jerk my thumb to add credence,
but my heart's not in it –
some are fooled by stomping, passion's

facsimile, not I.

So out of a dark auditorium
I guess at sweating faces rising up to me,
like a seductive water:
'Fall, we will release you!'
'Next time, next time I will do it,
I will release the astral body next time,
I shall float like a firework,
leaving the stage engines to trundle noisily
like tanks across the deserted theatre.'
We tramp the scaffold and mouth strange meanings,
but the scene shifts key again,
it's the wrong act, the ghost has walked,
somebody is tying up the plot, pointing
the moral or juggling with the ambiguities.

Out of deferred blood, clockwork mythologies,
Hollywood heart staging a comeback,
practice of extremity before the final take,
extemporised techniques of generosity
played out upon the screen that each projects,
pursuing, each pursued by his own treachery.
There will be no dissolution as desired,
but once again we shall stumble through
the dry tables of unfinished desire –

lessons to learn of the heart's division,
never understood, only by heart repeated
for friend's approving self-respect
and lover's prophylactic indigence.

Post-coitum you justified
the lack of what had been denied,
the story of your life paid out,
how stressed virginity made out,
locating primal sympathy
below the waist, above the knee;
accepting your depressive fate
prescribed for by the Welfare State,
whose kingdom now that it has come
makes all things bright with valium –
if sex should fester on the wing
it's painless to remove the sting;
impersonal, circumstantial, brief,
cathexis brings some light relief,
a para-sympathetic rage;
as rats in a genetic cage
are coupled to the sound of bells,
rewarded for their liver cells
by service to the human race,
by kindness in a human face,
by knowing human gratitude:
a button that will keep them lewd
connected to a slight device
re-engineers lost paradise
and proves that instinct needs no mate
if only one can concentrate;
for itching in the loins begets
species and singular regrets;
all that we need of fun and pain
the neural nexus can sustain.

Irrational belief insists
that somewhere something more exists,
what *it* is in the words below
it is impossible to know.
You looked for it in one-night stands
but all the pressure of strange hands
could not confirm that skin and bone
was heir to more than grunt and groan.
The nightly shudders were a start
at warming the sequestered heart,
with alcohol to feel less tense
relinquishing all innocence;
from bed to bed you dumbly rolled –
what else but mud might harbour gold?
Whatever grew by being repressed
withered again when you undressed.
Anticipation still requires
corroboration of desires;
the act itself in retrospect
is not as good as you expect,
by then, of course, you have released
all but the languor of the beast.
Caught in the flagrant act's delict
when mens was rea, conscience pricked –
yet who has ever gone to bed
without the face, if not hands, red?
No promises you gave and none
expected: it was all good fun
which like a mushroom overnight
swelled up, to wrinkle with the light;
as each unties the knots of slumber
one leaves behind a false phone number
and seeing a mirror in the hall
adjusts one's face – and that is all.

Each night you felt the same old sweat,
pursuing what you would forget
and after each had left his mark
of routine rutting in the dark
you swore that you would pack it in,
exist on Bach and double gin.
For all I know:
                      sex at first sight
dies in its moment of delight;
the moth goes dazzling to the flame
and touching shrivels to no name.
This doggerel's too long, too rough
and with that word I will rhyme love,
the consonance is incomplete,
but what the fuck, for who fucks feet?
Tetrameter or Knittelvers,
English by Greek, German or curse,
iamb or trochee, tum to tum,
all those dull spondees as we come.

I'm all at sea:
                your body's usury
extorts exorbitant interest, ruining me.

I long for touch of hands,
life-giving and life-healing
after years of cabin-cruising, lands
where our desires mesh
in deliquescent ivory
and run like tongues of water
upon the heaving estuary,
the golden dunes of flesh,
surf-flattered sands,
that will empillow you and me
to let us lick off weariness.

The deadly nightshade of your eyes,
what does it shelter, what does it hide,
of reefs concealed to wreck my pride –
must I then dive to oyster beds
and hold my breath, the lips to prise
for pearls, which I despise?

A cowl upon the coral of your mind
where I am torn to shreds,
those dark, green, underwater eyes,
whither now the unmoored craft has drifted,
    shifted ballast,
    its mast snapping,
    its shrouds swooning,
    its wheel spinning,

   its keel cracked;
  the ship is sinking
through the feathery rafters
of the forever dismantling ocean
into the depths of your being;
I stray about trying to unlatch
the lockers of the sea, to find you there
and make that catch.

Oh grey-furred galleon
listing like a gull with broken wing,
caulked hull and rivet notwithstanding,
a withered thistle stalked by the splay-fingered sun
where mermaids and embryonic urchins run.

Long litigation brought to judgment
against us;
                each word weighed
in the balance and found wanting.

As child, as widow, each promises
that come the solitary night,
after wearing a face like broken glass
we would cry into our pillow.
Thus days are endured, the ice-floes
of evening blur into darkness.

A passion slowly detached from
its specific object, like the retina;
or nail from finger: on such shreds
of feeling that of one's sanity
one hangs to catch the sun
will further tear,
                the wind will eat it –
we use our bodies to keep out the cold.

Chewing upon your words I let you drift
from my inquisitive hands,
you dissolved yourself into sleep,
and like the chrysalis affected death,
the personality disintegrated
into fragments, scattering away.
And as you sleep, I know
I would not have you hurt for all the world.

Here we might meet at last

upon a common plane of meaning,
for we have walked for hours
on a lost trackway in an unfamiliar wood;
without warning we should come upon
a clearing where the mist of dewed bluebells
had stretched taut on guy ropes the canvas
of our mutual incompatibility,
a compound habitation.

A prospect of far water you were to me,
my abstraction from you a shocked mind
like the tense ice breathed from bluebells.

Later I heard the sharp cry, like a sea-gull's,
from your heaving body, and, since
you requested me I should inform you
of your dreaming, I remind you now:

'I could not at all,' you muttered, 'make
this deaf man understand me.'

But I soothed you with comfortable words
and found a gentle explanation.

We talked in languages we could not understand,
striving a contract.
                    'Cast out fear,' I said,
surveying the civic dead, salvation
of black column, draped vase –
a package-paradise no resurrection
would be able to disturb.

We have re-trodden our first, incredulous,
dull way among the out-of-mind graves.
'You are affectionate!' As I might not
have been? As others weren't, perhaps,
mere snags in the stream. No tenderness?
An observation or approval – you repeated it.
Passport for further posturing?
                          Silent and cold
as moon beneath a rapacious gaze
you looked out on a world of loveless
litigation, like an indignant reptile,
coital wreckage mechanically pushed aside
to assume manners.
               Do not fear.
You are affectionate, aren't you? And
how should one answer, whose intricate
plotting sniffed only treachery, some
small commerce of mutual aggression,
ritual digression, paid for in kind?

Annihilation by love lies beyond
compass of the ordinary; unhinging:
disintegration of the well-worn self.

I descended to a world of spectres, but spoke still
in courtly love convention. Now I lose my tongue,
hear no more words, sounded out by radar,
each boom an aching nerve. Why,
like a lozenge on the tongue of death,
be eloquent? Can you taste my contours?
Can you recite me to myself, for I am
spilt out.
          The insubstantial web
of blistered stars hides the sucker, but
no succour, heaven unhoused, cobwebs
cover my eyes, you have taken hold
of my blood-pump like an entrail,
and have bled it dry.

I'd never looked on you before as might
some painter of that patient school that make
resemblances, but without flattery,
such sober journeymen as would not fake
ideal beauty,
                  such as train the eye
to see what is and in that find delight,
that seeing, do so first with second sight,
for whom appearance cannot therefore lie,
although they have no very recondite
philosophy
                  but manners and repose:
some worked-for discipline.
If I suspend my passion to indict
on grounds of sickening, quicksand jealousy,
that wears compassion thin,
with speculation blinded,
                              I discern
a grieving gentleness about your nose,
dark eyes that must be harsh to be polite,
most eloquently cold and taciturn,
as though what lurks within
will never come again into the light
but cowers, brown, and vulnerably bright.

To put this down, because it is an ache
as sharp and broken as a falling wing
might be of some white bird that could not keep
the sky intact, I transform everything
with my imagining:
                      such as: an ancient sailing ship

undeftly falters in a clouded lake
where reptile fingers somnolently snake
through moonlit caverns low and dark and deep,
and other fantasies like that.
                            But for your sake
I would return to study ancient skills
for making proper verse,
the old conventions, nothing there opaque
or brash, or without shape,
                            or brightly cheap,
but every day rehearse
some fresh perception with what modesty
I can to clothe bare feelings; catch what spills
from the waves of wanting when they break,
to be the guardian of your mystery.
                            This should disperse
those dark and unforgiving clouds of pain,
to fall as a refreshing, fertile rain.

As the fountain needs the cistern,
as the basin needs the well,
as the face upon the water
bends to break reflection's spell,
so, my love, I need your sadness,
    my misprision
    of your vision
of our elemental hell
through peculiar nakedness wrapped in silence
searching tongues can never tell.

As the wind upon the water
drowns its face to find itself,
resonance requires percussion,
as the voices in the shell,
which my organs of perception
and our culpable discussion
    faintly borrow
    from your sorrow
and my sensual deception,
shudder as a foundered bell in you buried,
where the tent of taut-drawn parchment
masks a strategy of war,
    striking medals
    in the spirals
where the heart hooves through the ear,
    where the arrow
    that will harrow
is imprisoned in the air,
    stretched on dusk,
    the drumming husk

tightening like frost into my fear.

Echoes from a hollow well,
broken pitcher from whose breach
stubbornness at last released,
    what we spill
    is with us still,
streaming there beyond our reach,
the sagging sail becalmed in agony not peace.

As your quicknail eyes engender
cramp within my walled-up cell,
    so I brood
    on solitude
you have shown me,
as an emblem of oppression
    in whose gaze
    conquest prays
with executive compassion,
    lust surveys
with blunted claws what it adores
    till it abhors,
    pity cries
    with tender lies,
in whose talons greed destroys what it desires
and cannot face the pleading
    in your eyes.

As all courtly love convention
images foment dissension
    with the real,
    yet I feel
as such as Troilus felt – the tension
and the vivid apprehension

of imagination's clothes,
when each betroths
the self to what it loves and loathes.

So these words of mine reveal
what these words of mine conceal,

nakedness is in the robes –

for my state is dry and sour
for my withered roots don't flower
for I dread your searching power
as those waters drown, devour.

AT WEST HAM SPEEDWAY

Why do I always think of making love -
which if I cannot, gets me really vexed?
Perhaps you're right – I have a one-track mind
that spots connections no-one else could find
on almost any casual pretext.
Nevertheless, these riders chase a hare
for all it's worth, although it isn't really there.

Our modern courtesy makes speed the lists,
that moon-probe being our most prodigious tilt;
we know it is a formal sort of phallic,
especially poetical smart Alec –
like almost every monument we've built
it rears its rounded snout towards the sun:
computers wink and tickle and we all have fun.

Pricking persists, although the stakes are cash;
each in the helmet of an astronaut,
with shining thorax, one-piece boiler-suit,
etherealising what we guess at brute,
they limber to their steeds to rein the snort;
our secret wish – to see them hit the dust:
I don't mean love at all, but rampant, bursting lust.

You knew that rhyme was coming, knowing me,
they should be pensioned off, so I have heard,
such rhymes, they make the intellectual whince, he
sees the issue laid for good by Kinsey –
it is a most unscientific word,

so shove it where dualities belong
and let me then continue with my Minne song.

They're slipped at last and all that hunger loose,
our favourite missed the throttle, his back wheel
spins with the fervour of atrocious verse,
he stalls – such taking off's precocious, worse
he could be queer at heart or intellectual:
the jeering crowd consider that he ceased
to spurt ahead because his clutch was not released.

Now in the spotlight's glare the other three
jostle for power. I come for the smell,
I'll be quite honest, something in the air
which they've kicked up makes light of my despair;
the final circuit now, there is the bell:
we know the winner almost from the start,
but it's the stirred-up cinders that have got my heart.

Finished, the cinder-track must now be raked,
could that be conscience or some sort of art
to smoothe the way for us to ride again
and is the penis really like a pen
that siphons off its inklings from the heart?
The hazard of the lover is to see
all that's about us quaintly, allegorically.

Excitement we're here for, the extremist spasm
of nine-tenth's boredom and the other…what?
The classic anaesthetic definition,
the pilot's motto; prelude – parturition,
a lifetime dwindled to one local spot.
And sex – is it a pastime of this sort?
Not so! For me it's something other than a sport.

They're off again. It's over. We relax.
It doesn't matter which one gets the laurel.
It is the rhythm and the motion which
prevent our noticing the rotting ditch
we're in. This leads me to explain my moral:
we must build bridges over that abyss,
the building of it, not the bank, is happiness.

Is this an image, then, of love, my love,
is this what happens when we are undressed?
You are the sort of person who could sense
sexual connotations in events
where men compete in power. I protest,
this is what happens when there is divorce
of sex from loving and you say: of course, of course.

Something we've coarsened of that former style,
a golden age that's always just outgrown;
perhaps the troubadour made smutty jokes
on sow-ear purses or the pig in pokes,
then harvested the wild oats which he'd sown
to call it cultivation.
                        Let hearts grieve.
Tickets will sell out, and our words will, well, deceive.

Forgive what follows, exercise of style
I cannot sanction, the oblique-sublime
of brokenhearted manners drawn in rhyme;
the old conventions mocked without denial;

the forms and precedents that put to trial
our naked bodies for some un-named crime –
can we defend the charge? It will take time,
which begs the question whether it's worthwhile.

Accept this jargon, this abusive swell
of artificial incoherence thrown
from deep within the shadow-world of hell,

where melodies of hope turned out a moan,
and high conceit a screeching Philomel,
whose bill is blunt with all that pecking stone.

Across the tumbled vaulting of my mind
flickers your dry tongue, bat in broken well,
residual stroking of untowered bell
to which the terms of owning are confined.

Eclipse of sense projects through shuttered cell
counterfeit shadows fixed by hireling stare
of dispossessing eyes, spider in lair
stiffens in sensing what it will compel;

impersonating figures, flesh I wear
developed to your objects of desire,

I print the negatives that you require;

the suckled victims ravened: so I fell
headlong on your behalf straight into hell,
and strummed the fibres of the tortoise shell.

My heart is haggard, like an antique hawk;
courtly conceit, part warfare and part gaming,
procured gaunt chastity chaste gauntlet, taming
the fettered phoenix, not to fly, but stalk

upon the pigeons in their restless dreaming.
Crestfallen falcon, epicene of prey,
before you mastered me I fell away,
ensnared by your decoy and naked-seeming

gentleness, to rise as fancy's gelding
above a playful hunter's iron glove,
a wrist I wildly roost upon with welding

clasp, an echoed pulse beneath the caecal hood:
beware the heart of passion, oh my dove –
brought to the lure, it has the taste of blood.

In salivating slime desire breeds
its monsters: hybrid, fossil fantasies
of vampire, centaur, sphinx, that mask what is:
the ravenous nymph that lurks amongst dark weeds

to prey on passing strangers, to impale
on darting hooks of vivid apprehension,
until engorged to maximum distension;

sapped; clasp relaxes;
                    sting is in the tail:

the grub respired through rough anal gills,
then drowsed to heavy, honeymooning sleep,
encased in sunlight-burnished armour; thrills

the alembic's golden image to assay
for chastity: from their embalming creep
sepulchral spectres, winnowed by the day.

Lovers learn lessons from astronomy,
to scan recessive vacancy for light,
custodial beacons, vigilant and bright,
that pierce the prison of anatomy

and pick the circuit's double-crossing lock.
My lens, like yours, through whose engrossing sight
each beams to each, took up the torch to write
the convolutions of the cardio-clock.

It was no fuse. Though sensual patterns glow,
they fade – in burning, ash alone is rifled-
no cooling solder binds together tight

these ciphers whose decoded orbits show
faint pulses of occulting rays that, stifled,
extinct, and distant, trickle through the night.

That sour, abrasive ghost tutors me still
to his vocation, thins me, unravels
wraiths, he folds on wrangling points of devils'

pleading to the last strands and coils of will,

combed, carded wool.
        That stool-worm in the bowel
has bitten trawling introspection's net,
and I obeyed his precept, jibbing yet,
put hairshirt habit on, took schoolman's scowl

to squint at verities,
       to fumble beads
of bladderwrack blown up by glow-worm's tail,
retort that eats, refining, soil: he kneads

my colloid spirit, – then the lithotrite
will crush – he draws out with his finger nail
the stones that ripen from my wretched plight.

Symbols for the speechless may catch reflection,
match it with patient facsimile of
me as I fumble to unlock your love
with words that bounce off you; their deflection

rebounds on me in fragments of shattered
glass, my daily ration, which I must hoard
and hold in hollow hands, a broken sword,
maiming, not killing – as if it mattered

much to your identifying expertise
re the resectable root of my pain,
that deep inside me I am bleeding under

the scalpel which your steady hand has drawn
across my entrails – either show I please

or else go through with your indifferent plunder.

My soul-scourer, scourge of ease, sap-like drifts,
if there's a soul, back through time's bottleneck
scored, not bole-graining sense; each splinter speck
wintering heart filters, sifts me, sand-shifts
me, from wilt and withering.
                              I lost heart
or root. Herd to leeward hedging, unfed
Pharaoh's lean cattle, flesh-fettered – veins bled
cracked stones the see-through flaws of being apart

at locks warrened; flows blood nor wine not, spilt.
Sour spelling neither gourd distills nor bile
uncurdles, but old rind and peel of guilt

garnered to fathom famine; while dozes,
though guarding, self-gnawing – squirrels its pile
for unfreezing breezes. All then closes.

Constructive lust in cycles of rebirth:
sugar in time and corpulence dissolves
in water, but your body nothing solves
of arcane intricate not run to earth.

Refused conduction leaves me less handhold,
foothold; touched like a flower by evening, eyes
of yours shut; I from stale foraging prize
cannot open a smile, by curfew cold.

You are asbestos to my crumpled brand.
In vain shall I more than myself acquire

and not be quenched by your indifferent hand;

shuffling the bars with antiseptic gaze,
to dunk once more in that refining fire,
you stalk through shadows where your fancy plays.

There is no moral to a double bed,
unless the point at which our lives divide,
unless the point beyond which I once tried,
a castaway, to cling to what you said

until you moved your body to one side;
unless a foot, a middle and a head
and fumbling hands, but what binds them is dead –
random the shock which brought us to collide.

Long months I've persevered, plumbing your gaze
to contradict unspoken loss of charm;
it seemed your eyes were ready to erase

me, sentries barring access to the brain;
I shut my face that no look of alarm
prompt you to ask: 'Why must you still complain?'

Cat, let me cradle you, sinuous blue
desires mounting like nightfall catwalk
vertiginous between us as we talk
cross-purposed on the grounds for being true.

Like first pale star your eyes home me to hope,
whose tidal indolence will gather mouth,
guiding false north the tongue, hands to true south,

yet from my grasping slip you, lost as soap.

Swept by my headlamp you reveal an owl's
stung reticence.
                It skulks upon the ledge
of darkness, your stray smile: the flotsam fouls

my rudder,
            now with furled up shrouds I dredge
these shadows where the nightmare's solving prowls
that draws me knife-like on my being's edge.

Dead nettle, my white incubus, your lips
have sucked my spirit dry of living juice,
I lose my breath within the tightening noose
of that facsimile of mouth that grips
me;
        I must undergo apprenticeships
of devilling to get the pincers loose,
my fingers sorely work to reproduce
warm flesh around the bone your jawing strips.

Twilight has steered me to the woodbine, where
my face is buried, that I may not see
your darkened, slowly spreading hood prepare

along the undergrowth its fatal strike.
You rise and turn your eyes expectantly -
what is it pleasures you upon that spike?

On mossy stones I tried to rub the hook
from me; allowed the water to caress

redundant limbs, as fresh and cold as cress
the mordant kisses of that shallow brook.

If it were only you, if we could look
into each other's eyes again to bless,
to give and to accept forgiveness,
to see the things anew which we mistook.

You sat in concentration, shredding flowers,
that breaking time, that endless, aching day;
over the hillside, where we stared for hours,

the shadows harshly crept, the sun severe;
you watched me try to bathe the hurts away
a thousand miles apart, an arm's breadth near.

I have been passion's wine-press for some friend's
analysis, a lover, and such lines
as these, and strained for each of them forced wines
to sample, drawn off me; promised amends

deferred while each to his appointed task
postpones a just and reasoned recompense
for labour, till the stubborn heart relents
and I can frame away the tragic mask.

Once more I've done it, beaten into rhyme
that you or you appreciate a scheme
of formal feeling hammered out in time

in dissipation of the sexual theme;
but I have passed the passion of my prime,
which has worn out like a dissolving dream.

He lived in notebooks for a year or two
recounting every inner anecdote
of mutilated aspiration; wrote
a treatise analysing what to do

which analysed the need to analyse
(appended), seminal for light it shed
on certain good in words if not in bed,
which ended with an epigram on lies,

applied to bed and writing: 'We invent
deliberate passion by defining shape
through limitation; action, not intent,

is fiscal, else inflation – no escape!'
His life, apparently, being so mis-spent,
he burned his books and turned, he wrote, to rape.

There was a fellow lyred his way below
for someone's body and a soul it sheathed,
whose well-turned phrases jaws of hell unteethed,
but could not disbelieve his eyes, although

well-versed in rules of rescue from despair –
a lesson on recurrent nightmare's drift
or looking back; the lady had short shrift
if cold bed crept, we feel, between that pair.

These ancient cautions on the wedlock spring,
what relevance to screwpen or to spouse?
For passionless connection's all the thing

resolved remorseless, than which bodies house
no more than current with its lifting wing,
and the brief flight such confluence allows.

The dying part of you is corked with lead
that no corrosive indeterminate
gnaw at your virgin logic in debate,
though acid sex has laid on you in bed

its lick-stone lips and sucked, till both had fed
to death on poisoned emptiness and bleached
a sudden self from selflessness, or breached
again the wound whereby the self was dead.

In search of satisfaction your soft tread
across stunned wildernesses of dismay,
where skulking appetite still stalks its prey
till all the pulsing flesh to dryness bled –

  'This clinging prophylactic leech,' you said,
  ' prevents the blood from rushing to my head.'

White fish pollute this dream all night; all night
along the wall the blind man's stick I hear,
who shall not find me though he stumble near,
whose empty geometric eyes indict

abstruse, unexcavated depths; the scales
fall off, like cloth; I gnaw white flesh that flakes
in wafers of gold leaves, sweet snow the rakes
of conscience have not levied into grails

of absolution.
                    But these fish are spent,
unmended, lank; sequestered rivers sap
their sinews, till the doctored cat of rent

and rat, that suns in borrowed reason, slap
the water at them, still in patterns bent
of want –
                    I hear the blind man, blind man tap.

Down some dank tunnel I was made to crawl
and lost my bearings, till I saw appear
a globe of radiance, a bathysphere
they were preparing for its maiden trawl.

Then I was hurried through formalities,
upset their schedule by my delay,
I swore no-one had pointed out the way;
they took the score of my extremities.

Down we were plunging, heavy as a stone,
the pressure made me breathless, I complained
but looking round inside I am alone.

The casing buckles, soon it will collapse,
and falling still, it will be overstrained.
I hold my breath. And wait. And something snaps.

A fall of snow would give this stone remorse
whose hidden tributaries still convey
all that one put behind one of dismay
that panted to unearth again the source

of yielding.
                      Tufted outcrop fades to sheep
in unseen echoed bleating. Dry as bone,
the wind's indifferences kiss the stone.
The air, if it had eyes, would learn to weep.

No, there is blindness on these rain-scarred fells
for broken hands are all the thanks you'd earn
to touch scorched runnels with a soft relief;

somewhere the rumouring of ocean swells,
but stop your ears too, that for which you yearn
would freeze the valley rivers in its grief.

Why is it bent upon itself, that tree?
Grief must have formed such gnarling attitude
or some repugnance gnawing at the root
that is the bane of all good husbandry.

Its back lay naked to the wind at large
for its caresses, all its self curled round
to south and seemed attracted to the mound
it grew from, with such dour, grey discharge.

Closer inspection proved some parable
of loving; an ambiguous flush of green
had rashed its bark, responding to the pull

of out and upwards, making more forlorn
the excrementing pressure yet unseen –
squandering whiteness for a black, blind thorn.

Another summer some will not endure
that now summon for passage their grey wings,
for nature has a way with dying things
that start in brightness, falter, are unsure.

I mean my loving and the knocks it took
this year's long falling – what else tore my mind
till I must prove weak senses like the blind
and take my motto from the twisted hook

I cannot loosen.
                      I shall pull it through.
They gather yet to hover and recall,
as I invoke an idle thought:
                          if true -

that fable in which restless essence all
moults old to melt new moulding – would we two
know why we grieve, one summer, for this fall?

Why must I garden stone for what
will ease this dry, inveterate pain?
There is no harvest here to rot
in all this rain.

It has relieved the breathless herds
that loiter on this treeless plain,
observed by these laconic birds
in all this rain.

Something you did not say, or said,
burns me with thirst like rodent-bane,
to quench it now will make me dead
in all this rain.

To irrigate I let my blood,
sluiced from each throbbing, emptied vein,
but cannot regulate the flood
in all this rain.

Harvest from stone, or love from you,
or desert green with sweetened grain:
three things that never could be true
despite the rain.

Mutations sprout, old-wives'
rodent ranunculi shrunk to pale spectres
like beds-foot physicians, transparencies
flecked with gore; bloodhound has
crowfoot scent at the cells' fusion –
swollen the belly of the telephone;
hysterical ejaculation
what nightmares of infertility breeding
as each breathes alone.

Oh what birdsong has been frozen
in sterile entrails of iced-up phone,
complacent wimple's pre-packed cellophane
on the soap sarcophagus
of an auspicious omentum – not drown
in the dangling bottle but all serenely
pendulous, concussed like a mole,
float like a mermaid in her haloed caul –
she's only sleeping, see where
the spore marks present a tentative scratching,
look how her ruff is goffered like candle-wax gills:
in this sort of case it is birth that kills.

The night outside gathers
like ganglions around the stars;
pin-balled by your expertise
some jerk their knees,
whilst one by one their organs
are removed in jars;
inquisitive spider, you rove,
with creepy cremasteric fingers,

invading milk and honey land
to find it moon,

and the moon-calf moaning love
with the surgeon's knife and spoon.

Leap, leap, leap in the womb
you may yet jump over the moon
and the other side of the moon
is blank
like the other side of the moon.

All spring I saw nature force
and groan into creation.

Listen, I said, if I lay me among the dead
with patience, who knows,
but I may be taken for a thing of nature,
a servant of earth, the sun warm me
to my dream of life, so I become a tree,
as I have always striven.
                        I risked it
and went first into my father's grave,
saw the flesh of me bound about bone.

Why did you come and cover me with stone?
I have shrunk so thin of this diet of worms,
besides, the voices in this chamber echo,
yours amongst them.
Now they say: 'Poor first-born,
why sweats it so long like a pig
in bed a-mornings, does it not heed
the bell calls us to our cages?'

In the long hours of expiation
I told them I took passage
through a tree struck in the night,
that yet had upon it some few last
shreds of the year just gone,
a stem that had been life to me,
that after the bones of the streets had been picked
by the sour fingers of state, sucked by the gold-filled
teeth of fire, was not put out to glow

all that the world imagines
for the dessicate fruit of this earthen

body that we are fracturing
on the wheel that moulds it.

With the dead it seemed I came home,
to an empty house only,
to await the arrival of those I lost.

Jagged edges of night, a can roughly opened;
along the occult precinct clings a bloated moon –
now prises the sun itself like a dehiscent orange
over the reduced rubble of strategic cities,
swaddled in expanding webs of light
where flushed-out foetus cradles,
gapes its blood-red mouth to be suckled
by fangs, after the fallen stars have stung.

The surgeon's moonly proboscis
sucks nectar from the dying,
waving like weeds in the tank,
ferns lathing their luminous
and green wraiths of glass.

So hot on so cold
all the trees this winter were charred black,
a sort of stroppy souls in self-imagined,
self-committed hells that lick the razor,
put forth fever, foaming at mouth,
blood and the spun floss of semen,
uncombed shoddy,
whose backward forward spring
shaves them to black bone and leather,
a mind burnt out
on the concentration of sheaves –
such that a child, orphan of shrapnel,
that played all night dolls and doctors
while they pounded the stressed concrete,
credulous questioning these ghosts of charcoal
their blistered lips, could ask only:

*Why, oh my ancestors,
do you break in leaves with no blossom,
what are you saying now,
for spring, I was told, was months to begin,
ancient to come as holidays...
is this the love the dead will bear me,
watching over us?*

                      *Have you come to deliver us,
did we dream the soft orchards of fruit-picking
and are you guardians of waking?*

Am roused by plucked strings
of the broken air;
                what is that mute beast of snow
creeps outside that my dreams have drowned out…
he sleeps,
        reach your hand into this pocket of time
to steal a definite meaning but make it gentle.

He wakes and where are you going,
but I hear the drip, drip, drip
in the withdrawn garden
that on soft feet pads silence:
                      give pardon
now in the hollow chambers of the tideless.
Drips what, then, drips blood and sleeps
in, in, in – whose: him I choose.

You have clutched that white mouse too long,
such blood you draw from its baffled heart
stains barely your purposes,
take another and another between exiguous digits,
ease the liquid from the unmetaphysical flesh;

he fidgets – who is to be let bleed next?

Why does that locust never learn
for all its slow exoneration of patient perusing
persistent glass that has crept a mind
on thin ice skating's perplexity;
it can prove no theorems on the diffident
ceiling, keep though it may quiet
the charred scrotum of the corner.

What the black bag may release of white
sweetness is yet dark; arms bow over a head,
hide a smile that guts darkness,
a mouth that will worry blood kisses,
unpurse with blue fur of unlodged voices,
limbs one may stroke in fountains
of black blood.
                    Therefore slip every time
my hands on the upside-down glass.

Loth to be crushed locust, let go,
go limp, loosen. From clutched sheets
shall the corpse pronounce fixtures,
across whose eye trails of unravelling serum,
washed pale by erasing waves.
I wait and can feel my wings prick
as eyes do with tears:
                    shall flutter
towards the quick stitching without malice,
be torn off with a pedantic extasy.

A million or more mouths to feed,
twist up towards me as the ground trembles

with armies the fleshless wrists
of supplication for bread.

I shall awaken to a mouth parched
with the dust of cobwebs: for what reason
steals my shadow when I lie still
over the ceiling towards me there
like a locust on glass turning for escape;
why is it scraped by weariness
from the wall to flutter here,
to the lipless mouth of my unbecoming,
in the grey web, ebb-echoing, ebb.

The darkness dripped
beyond the pane that separated our blank selves.
In the darkness together we lay alone,
you were asleep, your blue-wax body
unstamped,
                 the seals of my anger unbroken.

It startled me, the first chords
of questing or testing beast,
the pitch exact as the bursting of ripe fruits,
till I placed it as cats, guarding territories,
the spit and hiss of realities
outside our window –
more than a scratched record,
it was the wail of integrity
that cats articulate with brave immediacy.

Your blue body shrouded by tenderness
not in my arms
was soft as fungus, a mould on my thoughts
now searched by claws I drew from voices –

in chromatic ostinato
the pure fugue of this coarse quarrel,
a pizzicato bickering
on bodies taut as the breaking string –

it felt like an essential membrane, tearing.

You did not wake
but slept through the splintering of glass

between us till I too fell asleep
and woke to salve my sores against your back,
arched in slumber
round which I curled myself

while in the drained dawn
I imagined mauled cats

limping to some sanctuary
with no need to explain the hurts they nursed.

I dreamt our journey – darkness a clenched fist
that battered me. We rode our bikes as fast
as power would permit. I lit the night
from mine – it fell around us dragging, a full net
of urgency: we had to cross the pass
before the mountain-light that promised peace
was swallowed. Both the motorbikes might fail
at any moment.
                    As in love I fell
so deepened darkness, as a spreading stain.
At last we faced the steep ascent of stone,
approaching over, now we had to climb;
if we could conquer steepness we could claim
true passage through what devils could devise
to lacerate the keeping of our vows.
This was the crisis: if each could surmount
this obstacle I'd know our words were meant
in mute experience. I saddled fear
with love, to reach that summit, howsofar.
Both bikes were laboured on the twisting, steep,
half-blotted way, but you were forced to stop.
Though mine climbed surely, slowly, far behind,
I left it lying to offer you my hand
to get yours started. Up the sheerest slope
I pushed you (straining even in my sleep,
but never thinking to give up.) You checked
the throttle – from my power the engine choked
to life. You moved ahead into the sea
of black. I heard, though I no longer saw,
your now swift progress. Then I had my own
to follow on my bike, to reach and join

you. Steering to your streaming light I rode
towards your shape that loomed against the red
of sunset in familiar silhouette.
You turned inexorably round to wait
for me. I waved in triumph. Nothing back,
except a sudden fury from the bike
you had excited. I could not believe
what happened next, so blinded by my love:
you charged me down with that immense machine,
came straight towards me. As my headlamp shone
I saw your features, bloodless like a ghost.
You ran me down with palpable disgust,
and left me bleeding, with the bike to crush
breath from my body, reeling from the crash.
I only dreamt it and I must have wished
in dreaming that my body would be washed
by some remorse and tenderness, regret
if not great love for kissing me with grit
you pushed my face into.
                              Dreams do not lie.
Another scene: we both were naked, lay
together, you upon your knees, looked down
on me with pity, saying: 'What have I done,
here, let me succour you and soothe your pain
with this my nakedness.' I looked upon
that glowing intimacy that would heal
my broken spirit to a liquid whole,
in union. I saw the scalpel flash
behind your eyes. You peeled away my flesh,
ripped off each layer like an onion
and laid aside the pages of my skin
when you had read them, blankness in your eyes,
whilst I bled whiteness, milky in its ooze
of bitter ointment rubbed into the wound.

You were precipitated on the wind,
dissolving from me into clouds of white
that floated off and left the darkness wet.
Concupiscent requirements?
                              I dreamt
one further fragment: somewhere voices drummed
as in a cellar, voices that conspired
to plot some overthrow where none was spared,
and whether they or I the hunted prey
remained uncertain.
                         I set out to pry
their whereabouts. A secret passage led
me as the whispers grew. They said: 'You lied!'
and said it louder till I saw the glass.
They were my words, and this my voice's gloss.

I woke. A nightmare. Am I then bereaved?
The silence ached with motorbikes that revved.

Pigeons grown rank and fat upon the lonely love
of this grey city; now they bob and scratch
like brokers of our needing; stain the time-worn
temple masonry with their impurities,
that bring us back who strain
at broken versions of forgiveness.

The mid-day sky is worn upon this city's brow
like some frayed bandage of another conflict's
slow to weather wound, whatever pain is woven now
into the fabric of the bone.

The mid-day telling time of twelve reminds
some suffered blow to ache that presses heavily
on each sequestered reaching after stone,
to wear its greyness;
                            pigeons peck and scrape,
a restless rushing to possess, which those they chase
will not requite; it seems like rape,
and puts the females into fluttered flight.

A little child, in party dress, all white,
with sturdy, to-be-tried fragility
joins in this dance and whirls around to bless.

Now I observe they mean to mob the girl,
for she has fallen and the dance must stop;
the white is sullied and her palms are grazed,
and pigeons know no pity in their urge;
we may disperse inquisitive marauding and pick up
this child, the child in us, however phrased,

the dancing of all children that obeys
some greater principle than simple need.

The pigeons race once more in their familiar greed.

IN THE ALMOST DESERTED PARK

There's optimism for you – those young boys
fishing extenuated water, rods
that ginnle promise in the lessening air
woo what the packed exhausted stone has dropped;
      because the swans have come too near
that not yet disenchanted rascal prods
pitch-queering soap-white self-made rectitude,
or something like, for what the evening cropped
is knuckled to the falling-tethered noise
of starlings.
              Given, are not lightly stopped,
such moments, feelings which are not renewed.

Whilst in the playground where an only child
has tried all pleasures, wants at last to cry
but no-one hears him, sits upon the ground
and waits for night to scold the crocodile
      of crying at what cannot be found –
if he could tug that something from the sky!
Such insolence the world about him wears
that he will master heaven and revile
excuses, take the slipping stone as bride
as if a hand could gather up the smile
that has been winded from such slight despairs.

Come the long evenings after rainfall.
He kneels to smell damp earth,
                               runs yielding
fingers after the earthworm through warm soil,
lets no spade spoil
                  the uncovered fullness.

Are searched out like generations' past
unbroken hurts to dispose of, the heavy grenades
of sweetness to sustain winter.
                           One could lose head
in such discovery of secrets earth has kept.

Roots of gentleness bleed into his palm
what blind hands grope;
                 slow ache
of touching finds a firmness to dissolve it,
after which he fumbles,
                    while rain-fresh redcurrant
and the golden gooseberry flesh tremble with water
to his hand's swelling that feels them,
                             the promise
of tickled buds enlarging to the radiance
that is loosened over the landscape,
                               assuaged in quietness
after the soft plucking of caressing showers.

IN THE SMALL HOURS

The gates were shut. And no-one was about.
Locked in till morning when we could explain
how we'd been caught by curfew.
                                  Lights went out.
We hugged perfunctorily to ease the strain.
I heard a rustle, thought I saw a spark
or torch of some patrol that veered away
across the bushes through the deepening dark
that rose towards our cabin;
                            tried to shout
to prove we meant no harm but could not say
a word.
          The night was silent all around.
We did not speak, and tried to settle down,
folding our coats on the uneven ground.
You fell asleep.
                 I watched you as you dreamed,
your lips were moving, but without a sound;
your eyes were flickering;
                            but then they seemed
to open and to stare with unconcern.
You put a hand across to stroke my head,
but barely roused yourself. The strangeness grew
familiar at last.
                 Would it return?
The night wore on and nothing more was said.
In the small hours before I slept I knew
this was our home, of course, and this our bed,
this the great distance between me and you

this all the comfort that I could expect,
both for the future and in retrospect.

Entering, for the first time, a room
that will, for a space, be home,
you look from the door in the corner, inward.
It seems like prison, or inhabited
by someone else's emptinesses.

Perspectives change as soon as you settle,
you look from the centre to the door, outwards;
it is two different rooms, the second warmed
by habitual unstrangeness.
Whom you came with, to live as one
in borrowed house,
                         you give such twin being too -
once seen inward, full of blue corners
and angles such as night reveals,
which you never rub smooth;
then from the centre outward seen
towards the door, shut,
which to enter you had to open.

The last time you pass through
you will divest with sweeping glance
the room of you
              and restore its perspective inward
looking upon someone else's emptinesses
from the door.
              With whom you entered
can such gesture simplify
and make an end,
who came in lover and departed less than friend –
such things confirm us

hung like dead relatives on the wall.

So we made habitation,
colonised the inquisitive mysteries
of evening that lolled on the garden wall
like neighbours' cats, brought
through the blue window these nights
sleeving the far fruit trees,
left spaces that shrank
from our last touch of something weathered.

Strange noises fill the room
now you're not here –
the ticking like snow-flakes
that fall as star configuration;
a drowning man awakes
to understand the difference
your absence makes:

not here, not here, not here,
so it will burrow through my sleepless head,
and echo through this empty bed,
when I awake alone;
accustomed to my plight
as eyes get used to light
still shining emptily on emptiness
around this empty room
your presence touched
now touched by absent you
like water that has filled a valley town
where muffled bells pronounce
I drown, I drown, I drown.

I have no air
and must become amphibious
now you're not here,
more than the dinosaur adept
at adaptation, though as cold;
curled up, I wept
that you were wrapped in time's neat fold,
which shook out nothing
but unchanging place

and the impression only of a face,
your face, that holds
me in suspense awhile
and vanishes without a smile.

This ticking promises all this,
this and the end of promises.

And time stood still,
that afternoon it seemed
that what we'd built of loving had collapsed;
upon that hill
where time was not redeemed
our only words: perhaps, perhaps, perhaps.

So we must pay
for every slight deceit,
for every smile that withered to a scar;
for who can say
the other is the cheat
who knows too well: you are, you are, you are.

And time moved on,
we were unreconciled,
something divided us we could not break.
When you had gone
I found a lonely child
kept in a cavity of that iron lake.

They say: old as the hills,
the pattern we repeat
sustains a while then kills.

We say: superimposed,
the human element that runs
oblique defines a door by closed.

I say: my words persuade
love's possible with us again
my words betrayed.

You say: forgive –
my nature over-rules affection,
darling, I must live.

Therefore, old as the hills
again – a quick incision severs us
into our separate wills.

I gazed all evening on the level dunes
of moonless sand as though I thought there might
be some sweet flower still within the ruins
of love, that could be bruised to put things right.

Atropa belladonna I would pick,
if I could find it without you to guide
my searching fingers; that should make me sick
and cure the other sickness deep inside.

How should I know the poison without you?
Without your categories I'd mistake
some vivifying hip for it and brew
a medicine to exacerbate the ache.

You offer anodynes enough to heal;
I have refused them out of remnant pride
because to be alive I have to feel
morbidity devour me inside.

I could not find the herb that would annul
these feeble last declensions of the heart –
I had no other choice, then, but to cull
the dehydrated essences of art.

i

woke to a night peeled back like rind
he and his voice were lost
redundant syllables of an echo
long years trying to be kind
lathed like a replaceable appendage
on his own volubility
stunned by the sun
policing the cells of his forsaken
forsaken dreaming
through the familiar blue gallows
a tunnel where at this same root of night
the untransfigured tree
congeals blue in naked unfertility

ii

dog-like that is of shadows a substance
sniffed and pissed upon the stunted
territories of performance
one with the sneeze of every fitful
pick-up satisfied in the act caught grunted

a dog avoids mines avoids yours
detours unavengeable outrages
of disappointed expectation
its carnal knowledge untainted
acts of pure cognition
upon the instant deflection
pleasured at inevitable random

for ghosts abroad the temperature
of rooms of blood declines
dogs too scent the intangible
embodiment of distress the death
of spirit roaming at quest
for whom this is no paradox
but growl where great philosophers
flick their marbles of meaning
at tangents of wound horn

he that was dog but as domestic wolf
who badly handled guessed
internal bleeding drew back aghast

at the polished spectre of the bed
with the large marble in its mouth

iii

fed into inexorable labyrinths
of a familiar landscape corridors
to the petrifaction of water stairs
that climb upward forever to lead always
by deception beyond reason to the pit itself
bucket in the well and hand that turns
the axle and the last shut room
where to meet with obstinate revolt
the reasonable adversary against whose
contraries the most complete integrity
would be only postponed by a stalemate
never a deposing and the stakes a head
to this end he imprisoned himself

beyond consequences
                        annihilation
pre-empted by the terms of the bargain

then rose the unappeasable portents
of vengeance
                      seven fleshless cattle
fragments of the devoured moon
upon embrace clutching bones that snow
had clothed while the black swan
swallowed the moon and was absorbed
into the lake that stank of dead fish
from a white wound poured fog
out of the fog the ferry
on the ferry the figure in hood

not yet my minion not yet
but like the anchorite you shall observe
my love's paralysis
                      then I shall batten
on you
          wait I shall be there

Waves that are rooted to a blow-lamp spine:
I searched for meanings in the night-drunk street,
the no-man's land that fathoms yours and mine,
our war where conscripts drag their tethered feet.

This pill-box skull, parietal thoroughfare,
neurotomised by switching off the mains,
mono-amine oxidase inhibitor,
where stray toms libertine the occluded drains,

was shattered: light-bulbs sprouted leaves of glass,
injected buds, a fracture of flawed jade,
the urban blood-shot where our evenings pass,
mouth kissing mouth, the tongue a hand grenade.

Now if were spewed up on the sleepless shore
such fragments of excess, the leaning tree,
old paint wept by scraped kisses from the door,
it would reveal again that locked-in sea,

that sea where breathing does not mean to drown,
where essence of each other licks the gills
of even spasm, not exhalations drawn
from the stale scavenging of threadbare gulls.

They are dismantling the street.
Incense corrodes the air; night's
unseen tumour presses beneath the tight-
fitting cap of an evening heavy as lead;
seeded willowherb rusts with frost;
the spine is torn from a bed-
room, a fire-grate hangs shaggy, a
too-yielding root-socket; an after-
math of smoke festers like shame
through the damp rafters; the street
aches like a dislocated jaw, unhinged,
dumb like the victims of assault,
echoing like a deranged
mind its own relentless, interminable
self, some ineradicable fault
(this asceticism the logic of
conjecture: the street is jolted).
Cerebration proceeds along the rail-
way overhead wires that scalpel the sunset,
day parts like a nail
torn from a finger, reticulate
gauze of evening grows pale,
shattered like a mantle
whose gas oozes a dull refulgence;
trepanation reveals pigeons
bulging for home, the street jangled,
came to out of inhaled an-
aesthetic, bowing like a Chinaman.
Overhead cables fossilise surf,
an ice-pack of ancient moonlight
fell like the feathers of a distressed

bird into the shore-teeth, night
moves imperceptibly nearer as
a telegraphic glacier, let the sun shed
its velvet horns into the thicket:
lochia after a day's labour; the sky
crumbles like cheese, the moon dissolves
like a wafer, lamps moult their bright-
ness onto wet rails whence
the snake skids, the pavement a seal
under the blue snow, roots of snow
of an uprooted street that bind
the wound of the disfigured air:
footprint of dragged feet, as hunched
shoulders, the ancestral ghost, limps
sideways into the blizzard, trans-
parent as glass, into the habit of ice,
left rumours of a monster with soft hands,
that strained after human ways of loving.

Haydn, perhaps, hi-fi, will humanise
the rented margin of our intellect's
sustaining passions: why romanticise
fanatic science and domestic sex,
the one ambition and the other lies,
though finding poise in cultural effects:
a ceiling curbs the more romantic fakes,
the room with love or lorries passing shakes.

The taste in pictures is not mine, offends
the hard-won coming of my status-age;
such loneliness as litters my days' ends
swift one-night stands sometimes at least assuage;
concertos; gramophone; and wine befriends;
though beating wings make palpable the cage.
Sometimes there is a vision of disease
and sometimes merely pressure on the knees.

Shelley would have us live in the ideal,
yet verses do not usually pay the rent;
why are we still a couple when we feel
that what we saved together has been spent.
I like the sex I seek, it's no big deal
to bed a stranger with no sentiment.
I kiss, if I am honest, any lip –
and this is only a relationship!

There is method in randomness,
a landscape of ciphers, codes, allusions,
all things rank in nature move to their
appointed end, mourned and celebrated;
Spinoza kicks his Katherine-wheel
cosmology like a sewing machine,
farrowing the vacant universe
with the litter of mother god,
a pig on its side that grunts in the dark,
whose treadmill slaves we are.
Oh the night sweats…
my skin is friable, peeling off me
like bark – I am observed
for the discovery of papyrus.
Homo sapiens calibrated my jaw,
talked me out of food to pick
the stars off my skin like lice.
Who is this species that plots
heaven's ascendancy, that counts,
and doing so, they say, spills
blood?
      I will return to my own
worship, the spring-horn electrodes
clamped to my temples can send out
their black body signals' submarine
pulse. Let them search in vain
for a message, the dwarf is dead,
they hear only the echo of the
split atom; I shall be put in
a booth to chatter. They will
listen for evidence of intelligence,

measure frequencies, stake out a
palimpsest of language as layers
of explosion. Someone will write
up the mutations.
                      Homo sapiens
taught me to hate with controlled
aggression, his definition of
happiness; he invented love and
cured it with immunology. My god
has been defeated by drilled
legions and architects, he was
put in a vasculum and shaken, it was
semen that showered like snow and
settled, they called him a priapistic
Jack-in-the box, a prostate gland,
a lignum carcinoma. Seminal simian
semiology, victor silvestris. Never-
theless, those loins will be scoured
like devil's elbow, the fungus in his
groin devour the flesh and dead men's
fingers feed stones to the wind's
daughters when the tide pulls out
to the moon's orbit.
                      The strobile
scyphyus on a worn stolon gnawed
by shrunk lips of worms, his earth
a dry punch-bowl which the ants
shall inherit. Oh then the landscape
will bristle with the abandoned
hardware of symbols, the code locked,
the key corroded beneath caenogenetic
oceans in lunar neoteny, but who will
wade through the glossary of extinct
terms where we are deciphered?

THE WHITE LADY OF WAPPING

About the landings and about you stray,
drifting, cut loose from that grey sepulchre,
the sea, with my dark executioner –
his my neck thirsty spear, oh spare me, lady

        take away

your day-denying love, who have betrayed me,
draw no blood from this repentant spectre,
too many years of ritual have allayed the

        beast of prey.

What, will you harrow hell on my account,
for here we ravel echoes on the wheel
of dreaming, try to mend the broken seal –
come not too near, I know your breathing freezes,

        take your hound

away from me, your sort of loving squeezes
sap from the stone, a wound that won't congeal,
once you have made me drunk, no water eases

        till I'm drowned.

We have abandoned what we may have lost,
blindfold brought hither, that we truly see
the second self bring up the swallowed key

of open doors – but you would tear the hinges

                in disgust

from the black threshold where the sunlight cringes
at your face. Rather leave me, lady, lonely
that so ravished by you…take your sweet revenges

                on some other ghost.

Stringing together make-weight commonplace
is honest labour: it will have to do.
Wrenching however hard, I could not hew
from that remorseless stone a human face.

Drowning's another method, whose embrace
I made a principle, and called it you,
craving undifferentiated blue
to blot away all landfall without trace.

Perhaps I wrestled well beyond my sight
with Jacob's sparring partner on the hip;
perhaps looked back, was turned to stone, or drowned
in dissipating tides.
                      Through this long night
I've looked the other way, at last to chip
warm topsoil earth to break some common ground.

IN THE REPTILE HOUSE

Vexed by such parables of human fate
as cage's fretful indolence suggests,
where earth's wild fires smother in the grate
and ash accumulates in empty nests,

we watched instead those metaphors of vice
that took the blame because the human race
discovered innocence, lost paradise,
learnt mastery, but only to debase.

Though common ancestry were zoophytes,
reptiles cannot be emulous of man,
for whom they do resemble appetites,
that thinks no cruelty, being custodian.

We try to look behind their eyes, but see
forms that impel inquisitive disgust,
who may ignore the ignorant bestiary
that slanders them, personifying lust.

All have been emblems of some secret bias
that man has borrowed to perfect his quarrels;
the poet, perhaps in this the best of liars,
excused it as an exercise in morals.

The snake has suffered most from our excess,
'corrupts by subtlety, to crush by force!'
because man suffered for its sake distress,
the fangs of conscience and their slow remorse.

Chameleon, of all the reptiles dear
to passive poet, to lovers in their dolour,
for like the one he feeds upon the air,
and like the other often changes colour.

We paused some twenty minutes at this pane
to contemplate the predatory question
that mocks our species' specializing brain,
observed the patient plotting of digestion.

A habitat of circumventive glass,
four walls, a floor, and providential roof
through which administering fingers pass
the daily ontological reproof.

Two independent eyes surveyed the diet
that delicately fell into the box,
a locust struggling with the glass, unquiet
like a philosopher at paradox.

The insect beat its wings against the air,
that still resisted everywhere it flew;
we thought such partiality unfair,
though they could not hypothesise a zoo.

Engrossed by this primeval pitting wits
it came upon us how the world was old
and pitiless in murder; and acquits
each triggered tongue returning to the fold.

The locust, tongued in a lascivious kiss,
is crushed between unsentimental jaws,
which human sentiment may take amiss,

therefore we frame oppression through just laws.

The victim's only exit was the throat
of its competitor, that when it struck,
in human eyes alone appeared to gloat
upon the thing so lately out of luck.

IN GROSVENOR SQUARE

I have come out into November sunshine,
from desks and cabinets where I write up
the words of prisoners for their defence.

I am trying to unravel love and poetry:
both seem to want to stop the flow of time;
and social change, to speed it up.

I recall our rampage, to howl down the Embassy,
to break the power waging war;
to build a different world.
                        All crave,
yet fear, the loss of boundaries.
Is that what poetry does, break down,
break up, and build, all in one go? And love?

I try to still the hurt of wanting one
who does not feel the same for me.
                        He cannot hide
the constant strain I cause that wears him out,
trapped between excitement's lure, the unexplored,
no consequences, no responsibility,
and a belonging - that's what I said just now –
that frontiers test allegiances –
they keep us in, invite us out.

This whispers through me still
its sickly shine. I punish him in twisted lines
of rhyme that tie him in, and simplify his needs,

forgotten Shelley, Rilke, Blake,
growth-movement exercises,
self-help manuals on how to love:
do not possess, avoid dependency,
exclusiveness shows insecurity -
first love yourself and then you'll learn to love,
love-teachers warn.
                      I try to make it work,
but it's the same old wanting
and the passionate pain. Impossibility –
to change the way we love – can that be willed?
Or simply give it up and go our separate ways?
I chose the first, it hasn't worked,
as you can see from all this blethering.

At one o'clock the Fifth Cavalry
troop to the rescue, gathered on the white plinth
where lame democracy salutes the pigeons,
exhorting us to honour our obligations.

Four years now since we stormed the bastille
of the golden eagle in its corrugated glass eyrie.
Outflanked the constables and scampered through
the hedge that those who rushed ahead had flattened;
it hasn't yet recovered.
                          Bemused observer,
I baulked at cigarettes stubbed out
on police-horse flanks to make them rear.
Our men in blue linked arms on behalf
of John Citizen against the torrents
of lawlessness, who rushed them like rapids.

This afternoon the Union of Post Office Workers
keeps vigil over that war; it has entered

our souls, and in our dreams inextricably
intertwines the news with solitary inquietude.

The band now unrolls rousing introits to paradise,
snake-charming the serpents of harmony,
whilst coiled about them
the golden pythons of tuba bellow
like emblematic elephants.

Let some child sing:
The king sits in his counting house
with his intellectual peers
explaining all the failures
of the revolutionary years;
the queen is selling honey
to the starving and diseased.
And we... each sits alone,
to calculate our fears,
which by abstruseness are appeased.

For a moment the sun in the late leaves
has lifted me out of all this
and left me with nothing to hold onto;
that passed, and I must return
to the office.
                      I have solved nothing,
though I dropped that ornate utterance for once.

No doubt what happened here is more important
than angusto proelia lecto;
                      yet that too mattered then,
not in those words;
                a dead language suits
my abstraction of desire into a demon

stalking my every step.

I often try that cold and spurious art
of poetry, the moment made a monument;
here I have told the truth, at least in part -
about my failure in love.
                        Just what I feel,
with no pretence of precious poetry.

NIGHT CROSSING

'Are we to have from this some verses, then,'
you asked, because the gulls were scavenging,
with scant success. I scan the darkness. 'When
the larks that herald dawn return to sing,'

I answer.
        'Alaudidae, at least not
lullula arborea, don't cross the
Irish Sea,' is your reply. 'Would they be shot
that want to sing for joy?' 'Yes, probably.'

We cut into the darkness; the ship falls
and rises with the rhythms of a bird;
it throbs in catches with the seagulls' calls

across the black and echoing immense,
reverberating sounds of the unheard,
some voice of an unknown intelligence.

FIRST LIGHT

We shall expect punctilious ceremony
to crown the dawning with a new emotion,
who wait for morning like a comb of honey
that has been gathered from this punch-drunk ocean.

Thoughts you have tempered, like these grey gulls winging,
soar in the turbulence of this ship's wake;

all that we sail towards outstrips our longing;
islands loom up, like a familiar ache,

of some extinct volcano.
                        Now untethered,
the eyes accustomed to dissolving blues,
we may stand back and feel that we have weathered

a storm or two and have got back some health,
are even, as it lightens, free to choose;
the dawn we looked for has crept in by stealth.

LANDFALL

Like love itself, at which point it first scratched
the grey horizon, whether sea or cloud,
we were uncertain, till it was detached
from either and our vision of it cleared

to brute discoveries, inescapable
small truths of hangover, relentless scalp
that needs to make the echoes palpable
which had drummed up through intermittent sleep.

No way not to dock and make acquaintance,
the self dwindled to restricted handshakes,
best face forward, time past for repentance;

self-exploration still remains unfinished;
subject to timetables, the silence breaks;
in the grey light our restlessness diminished.

HELEN'S BAY

That distant ship seems stuck on the horizon,
each time I look away it seems to move
an inch or two with patient, breathless motion,
but stared at, like a needle in a groove,

it is the wave's sane rhythm which unscrews
its coming nearer. As my mind had grown
as blank at first I thought that for his dues
my grey tormentor, come into his own,

made headway. It was just a ship. You stood,
your eyes absorbing all the sea's strange green,
although it did not darken, said, 'it's good

to have you with me...Ireland seems benign,
if not quite home...,' fell silent at the scene
of something somewhere we too much define.

AT INCH ABBEY

So, it will come to this for our love too;
I plead the stone this morning to retain
all my life's focus narrowed down to you,
resisting time, that I may weather pain.

Tumbledown centuries have blurred what prayer
confided to these unrepeating stones,
whose promises inherited the air –
I hear the whispers chanting through my bones.

We stand together now and nothing say:

I read again where thought must be extreme –
the frost must succour me lest I betray

some sudden loss of faith.
                              I turn once more
to catch the echo of an ancient scream
that howls forever at a silent door.

TYRELLA STRAND

If love had substance it might be like this
green olive the tight shore-line sucks and gnaws
upon to chew out heckled bitterness
for relish; steeping marble ocean taws,

brings up to scratch a hiding, branling scurf
from the scrubbed litoral, but not to slacken
sand's seething backwards through bared teeth of surf,
the dunes that tenant only saline bracken…

it could be that, or any other clash
of unseen urges waving through to shock
the almost uninhabitable…
                                      rash
assaulting you, I almost understand:
my teeth have crumbled underwater rock
that I cough up as purifying sand.

ARDGLASS

Too many ruined chapels, heaven-trawlers
wrecked on this blue headland, remind that we

are running out of time to disenthrall us –
all afternoon we drive beside the sea.

These tweezer streets have plucked a living out
from puckered waters, fended off marauders;
they face the harbour, walls of their redoubt
against invasion. Respecting borders,

they hold the land on this indenture torn
from water to prove title, and the terms
of time as tenure; time runs and will warn

tenants that their security reverts
to ultimate possession: which confirms
that lonely landlord who will feel our hurts.

Stopped on a bus by British soldiers
holding guns; another time, the same,
pointing straight at us, as we drove behind;
were in their sights:
                        not London this.
I know that someone's terrorists
have killed the innocent; I do not understand;
how could I see this lack of comprehension
all around, this grasping, violent hate,
and not interpret it as personal?

I do not shoot, I have no bombs,
perhaps could talk a city down
with disappointed love;
I stay my hand, you are beside,
for once you smile, you seem to hold me dear,
as though we, reconciled, could find
a way of living without fear.

Put on a uniform and grab a gun,
you are protecting freedoms, shoot at will,
and this is Ireland,
where they simply kill
to satisfy integrity.
                      And you and me
in all this senseless killing?

We shall see.

Black kite,

that can so cut
the sky in half
with one huge sweep of hunger,
soar a little longer
over what you hover,

you will see
the glacier of procreation fast asleep
in that steep crevice of constraining lake,
time's bodice of eternity.

       You cannot wake,
not her, nor us,
nor by your haver force

such self-composing liberty of peace,
how much you dip and dive and thrust.

Frost has stretched its hand over the water

to warn the truant
not to tread
on golden grass it tarnishes.

Webbed fingers clutch a branch
bind it
to secret otherness of the releasing air.

That sun
playing skittles down the elm-caryatids
has trailed his hem over the creased water,

as it were a fountain
locked by night
he courts with slow praises
now will flow into the ungestured silence.

Put down yourself, put down,

for these healing fingers
immeasurably to lay out.

Sleep thumbs your eyes,
so many unread pages to erase –
the old king carried into the hillside.

Like soap
I take your legs between mine,
who must live our death closely,
                intertwine
these not to be eradicated rancours,

till our bed
could never lose the hold of the bindweed.

Let me no dew dislodge from your blue head
nor tremble it
that the hawk-moth pilfers
for sweetness
                into the drenched dark
unfurl us with that one white cup

that quenches the cold with snow.

AN AMATORY ELEGIAC EPISTLE

Sex, I said, has indissolubly linked us.
At least till after waking
when its many-loined creatures pale
before the advancing queues of revenue
and marketing men, and we subdue our desires
to the quiescent cages where they may snore
or fester till the dusk unlock again
the lunatic vagueness of our unquiet bodies
on the leash of the imagination of infinities.

It sounds what one knocks off
to sweeten or procure seduction,
flimsy and accusing as a dream
when you set about untying the strands of sleep,
breaking out of them with a mechanical promise
to return, looking at a face that does not launch ships
but might invoice orders of containerisation
and study bills of lading.
                                    They will pursue you,
sometimes to the ragged strains
of dislocated heartburn, sunsets
laden like buses too jammed to request,
the blue ice on the pavement aching to be born.

Heloise wrote to Abelard from the cloister
in some confusion about her proper role,
heaving among the sisters like a wounded queen.
For insects there is no such problem;
to avoid chaos and establish workable identities

is the goal of civilisation; as all the industry
of colonies and hives.
                        I know we assume instinct,
where insects respond with efficiency,
spared the delusions of powerless power,
queens in yards and decades of black crepe;
a faultless algebra, a chess projecting
from first principles some stale-mate we abhor,
having no sense of the individual's isolation
from its function, cannot despair of lost identity.

She wrote to him, with all the details
of her loss, derision and collapse,
his sister-daughter-wife,
spun cobwebs of desire around the convent,
roused by the tremors of her echoing self.

We two sat in the departure lounge,
heard the honeyed voice of the hostess
proclaim our separation – to Ireland you –
like the indefatigable music of a waterfall.
In such moments where a thing is stretched
we meet a certain truth of gain and loss:
not so much each other, as the furniture
each provides in a vast and empty transit lounge,
to forget where we have been and go again.

For it is as painful then to think of Heloise
as to play over one's dreams on waking,
since departures, unlike thieves, and is sex theft,
give better title than they got,
as we are better when we are bereft?
                        Therefore I wonder how
the shadowy space will creak when you're not there

to fidget in it.
                    Heloise found love a trouble –
individual insects thrive without it;
elephants, being bigger, become rogue like us,
begin apocalyptic treks for water
such as in humans conceive a fall of Troy.

I can sympathise:
                    along the neon, vacant
Cromwell Road, tranquil and suggestive
as the mind of a sedated psychotic, my thoughts
wandered so, drawn back to the faint winking
of a plane that could have been yours,
firmly on a plane myself whose determinants
were calculable and would bring me home.

This separation gives me some relief
from you and thereby causes pain to me
because I do not like to like to be
alone.
        And is it true, therefore, that sex
has bound us together, beyond absence to disturb,
gently enhancing? That couple mixed
the carnal and divine, and you and I swap
incompatible paradigms that not even you
with your eye for an elementary error of logic,
unlike Abelard, can disentangle;
                              nor I,
with all my rhymes, can weave into a pattern
we could wear.

When we undid ourselves for the first time,
each experience of each a bruised flower,
the crushed being of your body free to roam,
free to escape like smoke, your silver hair
got in my eyes.
                    It was not the shock
of atoms I expected. Ghosts of snow
we woke together into a partial thaw.

It was to wander through a lost valley,
to blunder perturbed at uncertain guesses,
to make much of the chance exclamation,
to verify distances, constrain loss,
to come out puzzling where the dead
had really gone, whose bodies, not like ours,
were known only by stone and gravel.

No form of nature, almost into stone,
we are not torsos twined beyond our tongues;
trodden into the loam that rain is eroding,
the flaked colour of your hair and eyes,
these stones may be read off from the earth
as a Braille now by those of us blinded
who belong to succeeding generations.

Unlike flint my body will dissolve itself,
my mind filter at last into the root that now gnaws.
All that will remain, and that haphazardly,
will be words shaped for some purpose.
I call that comfortable consolation – what is a grief
to this landscape that fears no change.

Enshrined in the temporary grave of being,
it will be broken open by roots let down seeking,

as then I smelt the hawthorn in bewilderment
and clutched to own, but simply cannot learn.

HALF-LIFE

It had been, you said in retrospect,
a timeless day.
                     And now we let the boat
inquisitively bite the lip of the indulgent
whirlpool, going round in circles, jaws
not gnashing here or otherwhere for all we knew,
lapped us like the embrace I was postponing
as I could put off measured proofs of how remote
might be your thoughts from me,
                                   my hand in yours,
and what, if anything, such things denote.

Could it, playing my usual sort of fool,
with which I strain after faint stars,
untenanted cobwebs day brings a broom to,
be possible we are rocked here on the echo
of that theoretical outburst…
                               Almost I had you
by my whimsy, but went too far, for, and before…

how could you take it, other than serious
enquiry, to be dealt with squarely by slow
paring away of what the incurious
take by proxy, preferred to the various
rebuttals of transience you know…

I offered to walk the intransigent water
towards you;
                   your smile darkened, cast a shadow

that tugged a root from the so near to unfathom
water, or cut the tide like a swallow.

We have looked lately on a landscape
blurred with meanings we cannot match;
mortal experience, maybe, beyond
the scope of speculation to make permanent;
something dissolved of our togetherbeing
like the dead under the dry tongues of memorial.

Striding together
through a landscape of tangible aches,
we were mapping what to each other
we had been, exploring country
under new rulers. But it was now too late.
We could only count losses and bury the dead.

We move in knowledge of the space between us.
Fear, or pride, or the only lonely self-imprisoned
self has slandered you in me
till we will never again know that first place
of our soft undoing. I was a fool to think
our bodies built a bridge.
       If only
I could feel the wholeness of your being
and set you free;
    if only I could say, if only true,
you are that part of me which makes me whole,
you are that whole that is not part of me, -
such that my sensual imagination grow austere
where you have touched me;
        like a tree's that's nourished
in the temporal sun, so that the rod I made
of loving you becomes a living branch again.

Nothing, I know, can ever cross the gulf
that makes us two, but seeing suddenly
the fall of snow, I sense your seasons'
secrets, unimaginable as the snow –

and strain with every strength in me to let you go.

This is the time of year that best accords
with my sterility: the longest night
swallows the day whose white fog has erased
those special images my spirit hoards
of your brown gentleness that is debased
by every slogan.
                 I can only write
with frozen fingers forced to expiate
something too much desired, come too late.

Still I remember that first Whitsuntide
together, spent at Hampton Court. I had
some vision of a meaning, yes, obtuse
in definition, so you may deride
my imprecise semantics…
                          what's the use,
when I am honest what I wrote is bad;
enough of lies, now let me say it plain:
it is not you I love, it is my pain.

Whitsun – the blood that warms with sudden singing
in saddened ears betrays us to our senses.
I took our fumblings, our unfurling griefs
not for themselves, a tentative beginning,
but as a creed to beggar all beliefs,
a principle in broken-down defences,
a faith in nakedness.
                     I must enquire
what put out tongues of Pentecostal fire.

In fact, of course, I cannot love at all;

I want but do not want to want; and nurse
the shame as pity; like a church I spread
doctrines of love by will: strictures of Paul
for whom real life would come when we are dead.
Both writing letters,
                              hoping to uncurse
that self-originating drought we make
by loving only what we cannot slake.

Is love the fruit of our imagination,
can it be willed, is there a separate soul,
that aching vestige born of sex and sin?
Or one long sexual hallucination
dreamt the disparities of hell and heaven,
deluding us to think we could be whole
again? How could I know.
                                For I have lost
the wasted vision of that Pentecost.

To hold you in my arms, to hold
your hand, to put my lips on yours,
not in a heat of I will have my way,
but in a loss of hunger, searching out
your hurts,
                        to let you float
through all you are,
and still to want to hold you in my arms,
to say to you how much
I want you mine –
but then to say:
I will not hold you tight,
I will let go and love the loss of you,
into that purity where I must fall,
into a loss of smell, a loss of sense,
I will be patient for you,
though it seem like death,
and wonder what we'd have to say
if, so immaculate,
I did not try to have my way.

Post-coitum you justified	04
Sleep thumbs your eyes	89
Stopped on a bus by British soldiers	86
Strange noises fill the room	57
Stringing together make-weight commonplace	73
SUCCES D'ESTIME	1
The darkness dripped	44
There is method in randomness	69
THE WHITE LADY OF WAPPING	71
They are dismantling the street	66
They say: old as the hills	60
This is the time of year that best accords	99
To hold you in my arms, to hold	101
TYRELLA STRAND	84
Waves that are rooted to a blow-lamp spine	65
We have looked lately on a landscape	97
We talked in languages we could not understand	11
When we undid ourselves for the first time	93
Why does that locus never learn	42
Why must I garden stone for what	34
woke to a night peeled back like rind	62

TITLE AND FIRST LINE INDEX

All spring I saw nature force	37
Am roused by plucked strings	41
AN AMATORY ELEGIAC EPISTLE	90
And time stood still	59
ARDGLASS	84
As the fountain needs the cistern	15
AT INCH ABBEY	83
AT WEST HAM SPEEDWAY	18
Black kite	87
Come the long evenings after rainfall	52
Entering, for the first time, a room	55
FIRST LIGHT	81
Forgive what follows, exercise in rhyme	21
Frost has stretched its hand over the water	88
HALF-LIFE	95
Haydn, perhaps, hi-fit, will humanize	68
HELEN'S BAY	83
I dreamt our journey – darkness a clenched fist	46
I'd never looked on you before as might	13
I gazed all evening at the level dunes	61
I'm all at sea: your body's usury	7
IN GROSVENOR SQUARE	77
IN THE ALMOST DESERTED PARK	51
IN THE REPTILE HOUSE	74
IN THE SMALL HOURS	53
Jagged edges of night, a can roughly opened	39
LANDFALL	82
Long litigation brought to judgment	9
Mutations sprout, old-wives'	35
NIGHT CROSSING	81
Pigeons grown rank and fat upon the lonely love	49